COMPETITIVE CHEERLEADING

BY BETHANY ONSGARD

CONTENT CONSULTANT

Pauline Zernott
Spirit Director and Coach
Louisiana State University

SportsZone
An Imprint of Abdo Publishing | abdopublishing.com

ABDOPUBLISHING.COM

Published by Abdo Publishing, a division of ABDO, PO Box 398166, Minneapolis, Minnesota 55439. Copyright © 2016 by Abdo Consulting Group, Inc. International copyrights reserved in all countries. No part of this book may be reproduced in any form without written permission from the publisher. SportsZone™ is a trademark and logo of Abdo Publishing.

Printed in the United States of America, North Mankato, Minnesota
082015
012016

Cover Photo: Albert Cesare/Odessa American/AP Images
Interior Photos: Tammy Shriver/Times-West Virginian/AP Images, 4–5; Shutterstock Images, 6, 13; AJ Mast/Icon SMI 747/AJ Mast/Icon SMI/Newscom, 8; Seppo Sirkka/EPA/Newscom, 9; Phelan M. Ebenhack/AP Images, 10–11, 12, 29; Larry C. Lawson/Icon Sportswire, 15; Joerg Carstensen/DPA/Picture-Alliance/Newscom, 16–17; Joe Nicola/Southcreek Sports/Icon Sportswire, 18 (top), 21; Gary Coronado/ZumaPress/Newscom, 18 (bottom), 22–23; Leonard Ortiz/ZumaPress/Newscom, 19; Chris Matula/ZumaPress/Newscom, 24–25, 26; Michele Eve/Splash News/Newscom, 27

Editor: Mirella Miller
Series Designer: Maggie Villaume

Library of Congress Control Number: 2015945866

Cataloging-in-Publication Data

Onsgard, Bethany.
 Competitive cheerleading / Bethany Onsgard.
  p. cm. -- (Cheerleading)
 ISBN 978-1-62403-985-0 (lib. bdg.)
 Includes bibliographical references and index.
 1. Cheerleading--Juvenile literature.   I. Title.
 791.6/4--dc23

                                        2015945866

CONTENTS

ONE

CHEERING
BASICS

Most cheerleaders we see on television and in movies are cheering on a football field, but that is not the only type of cheerleader. Some cheerleaders take their skills off the sidelines and onto the playing field at cheer competitions.

At a cheer competition, teams of cheerleaders from across the region go head-to-head. Each team performs a two-and-a-half minute routine set to music. This is the official time limit. Routines can be shorter, but then teams showcase less talent.

These routines combine dance, tumbling, acrobatics, gymnastics, and traditional cheerleading skills, such as jumps, into one performance.

Most performances include pyramids, flips, and high-energy dancing.

With the help of a coach, each cheer team picks the music, choreographs the routine, and practices for months before a competition. On the day of the competition, teams perform their routines in front of a packed audience and a panel of judges. Routines can be just as fun to watch as they are to perform.

Each competition is different. Usually teams compete in one of six categories. Level One includes the youngest performers, and Level Six has skilled high school cheerleaders. After each team has performed, the judges announce the winners in each skill level.

The top teams are introduced at an awards ceremony, and trophies are handed out.

A group of elementary-age cheerleaders waits backstage for the results after a competition.

THE COMPETITIVE CHEER TEAM

Similar to cheer squads at games, competitive cheer teams are made up of girls and boys of all ages. Teams can vary in size from 6 to 36 members. Some competitive cheerleaders get their start as young as three years old.

There are many competitive cheer organizations across the country. Most organizations have teams for young kids all the way through high school-age cheerleaders. Some people cheer competitively in college too.

Many cheer squads are called coed teams.

TWO

HISTORY OF CHEERLEADING

Cheerleaders have been on the sidelines raising team spirit since the early 1900s. But competitive cheerleading has only existed since the 1960s. Now people come to events to cheer on the cheerleaders.

Cheerleading competitions began with college-age cheerleaders. Starting in the 1960s, the International Cheerleading Foundation ranked the top-ten college cheerleading squads on their acrobatic skills. The top team each year was given the Cheerleader All America Award. Cheer squads wanted to win this award. They became more competitive. Teams began to include more gymnastics, dance, and acrobatic skills in their routines.

Cheerleading has changed a lot since the early 1900s.

11

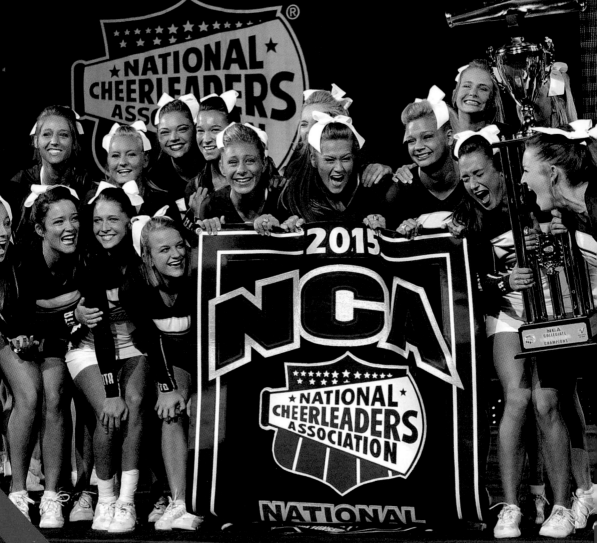

Cheerleaders celebrate their win at the end of the NCA Collegiate Cheer and Dance Championship.

Many teams compete in each cheer competition.

Ten years later, in 1978, the Collegiate Cheerleading Championship aired on television. Everyone who tuned in saw jumps, flips, and pyramids. People saw the athleticism behind cheer competitions. Competitive cheerleading quickly became more popular.

THE FUTURE OF COMPETITIVE CHEERLEADING

Cheering competitions are not only for college cheerleaders. Teams of all ages practice and compete. Most cheerleaders start at a young age. After years of practice, they compete in high-energy routines. More than 200,000 athletes compete in cheer competitions each year.

STUNT CHEERLEADING

Cheerleaders show strength, agility, and skill when performing their routines. Some people argue whether or not competitive cheering is a sport. The STUNT program was developed to help prove it is. Approximately 500,000 cheerleaders across the country use the STUNT program to showcase their skills. STUNT focuses on partner stunts, pyramids, jumps, and tumbling.

Competitive cheerleading is also becoming more popular with viewers. Competitions are shown on television. People pack the stands to watch squads live. Sports fans tune in to ESPN to watch cheerleaders compete, just like they watch other athletes.

A Level Six stunt team competes at nationals in Portland, Oregon.

THREE

PREPARING FOR A COMPETITION

Competitive cheerleaders spend years improving their cheer skills. By the time squads compete in Level Six competitions, many are flipping their way across stages. Before teams can compete, they need to perfect their routines. Coaches choreograph most routines. Sometimes they hire a professional choreographer. Older squad members also help create challenging routines.

Choreography is a creative part of cheerleading. Each move in the short routine is important. The routine must grab the crowd's and the judges' attention. It also needs to include pyramids, tumbling, and stunts.

Cheerleaders practice their routine after being taught the steps.

PERFECTING A ROUTINE

Cheerleaders spend time in the gym. They build strength to lift their teammates and form pyramids.

Teams often film their routines. Then they watch the tape and point out any mistakes.

It takes more than a few practices to get everything perfect. Many teams practice every day the week before a big competition. Practices can be up to three hours long.

By the day of the competition, every step and stunt should be in sync.

ALL-STAR GYMS

Not every school has a competitive cheerleading team. Cheerleaders can join all-star teams. Organizations and companies run all-star teams. At national competitions, all-star teams cheer in their own divisions. They do not compete against school teams. All-star gyms give more cheerleaders a chance to practice, cheer, and compete.

Competitive cheerleading does not have a set season. Most cheerleaders practice all year long. Teams usually meet two or three times a week. Closer to competition season, teams meet more often. Competitions begin in the early spring. Usually each team competes in three to five competitions each spring. Scores from regional competitions are tallied. The winners go to nationals. National competitions are held in April. This is where the best of the best come to compete.

An elite team performs at nationals in Houston, Texas.

GETTING TO COMPETITIONS

Most teams need to travel at least a few hours for competitions. In the United States, two of the biggest national high school-level competitions are held at Walt Disney World in Orlando, Florida. Smaller, regional competitions happen all around the country. The night before, cheerleaders make sure they have everything they need. Uniforms, snacks, and water are all important. Many teams travel by bus. The squad uses this time to go over routines and build team spirit.

A team practices its routine before its competition.

FOUR

JUDGING
COMPETITIONS

After months of practicing, competitive cheer teams get the chance to show off their skills and talent. Teams from across the region gather at an arena to perform their routines in front of judges. The teams start their music and walk out on stage. All their hard work comes down to a two-and-a-half minute performance!

Judges look for specific things during routines. The timing for all the jumps must be precise. Every team member's fists must be closed and pointed in the same direction. Dance moves must all be coordinated. Each cheerleader's voice must be clear and strong. Every cheerleader must land with his or her feet together after a jump.

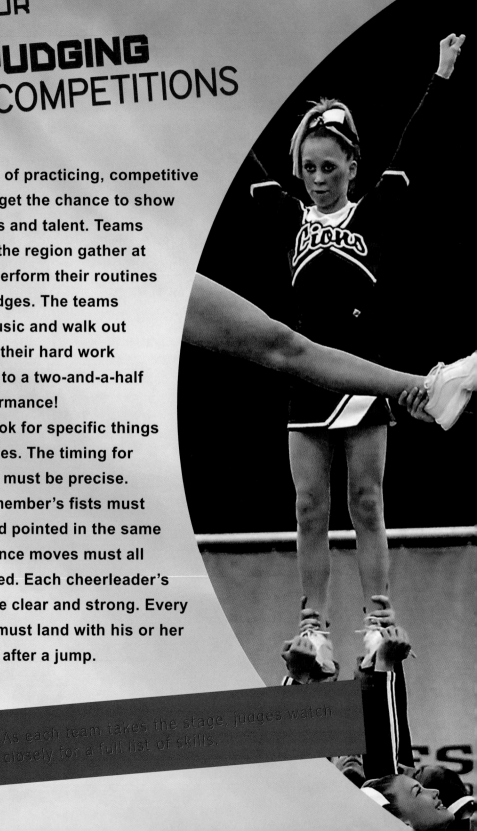

As each team takes the stage, judges watch closely for a full list of skills.

It is important for cheerleaders to have fun during competitions.

Judges are usually former cheerleaders or coaches.

Most competition judges were once cheerleaders themselves. They have been through competitions before and know what it takes to win. The judges have done the flips and jumps. Judges also receive training on how to rate teams. They can tell when flips are not in time or when a dance move is offbeat.

Not every point comes from technical skills. Judges also want to see a lively routine. They rate teams on how creatively stunts and dancing are mixed in a routine. If the crowd is having fun and cheering, that also means more points. Most importantly, the judges want to see the team having a good time while performing. Cheering is competitive, but it is also fun!

HOW TEAMS WIN

The judges tally the scores after all teams have performed. The top three teams are announced at the award ceremony. In some large national competitions, squads of all levels compete. Up to 10 or 12 teams are announced as winners. On the day of the competition, the team with the most talent, a solid routine, creativity, and teamwork wins first place. The crowd goes wild when the winner is announced. After months of practicing, the winning cheer squads have a lot to celebrate!

GAME TIME COMPETITIONS

Most competitive cheerleaders perform acrobatic routines. Some cheer squads also take part in Game Time Competitions. During these competitions, squads show how well they can lead a crowd. This is similar to what they would do at a sporting event. Routines for Game Time Competitions are shorter. They usually only last one minute and fifteen seconds. Game Time Competitions are a great way for teams to show off their school spirit!

The winning teams scream and cheer in excitement!

29

GLOSSARY

ACROBATIC
Performance that uses stunts such as jumping, balancing, and tumbling.

AGILITY
The ability to move quickly and easily.

ATHLETICISM
Being good at games and exercises that require physical skill, endurance, and strength.

CHOREOGRAPH
To organize dance moves and create routines.

COMPETITIVE
Wanting to win or be the best.

COORDINATED
Working together smoothly.

SQUAD
A small group doing the same activity, often a physical activity.

TECHNICAL
Using skills that are specific.

FOR MORE INFORMATION

BOOKS

Gassman, Julie. *Cheerleading Really Is a Sport*. Mankato, MN: Stone Arch
Books, 2011.

Webber, Rebecca. *Varsity's Ultimate Guide to Cheerleading*. New York:
Little, 2014.

WEBSITES

To learn more about Cheerleading, visit **booklinks.abdopublishing.com**.
These links are routinely monitored and updated to provide the most
current information available.

INDEX

ABOUT THE AUTHOR

Bethany Onsgard works in publishing and spends her days reading, writing, and exploring the outdoors in beautiful Portland, Oregon.